TRAVELS IN A YOUNG COUNTRY

DISCOVERING UKRAINE'S PAST AND PRESENT

MICHELLE LAWSON

MEDLAR TREE

Cover design by Jack Williams and Allie Lawson.

Cover photograph by Terry Dolman.

CONTENTS

PREFACE

This book was conceived during the #WritersforUkraine initiative by Activated Authors in March 2022. Motivated to take part and donate to the fund, I gathered material I'd written during my travels around Ukraine during 2018-2019. Those journeys were part of a search to find what, back then, I believed to be Polish family living in Western Ukraine. What I discovered was astonishing, although that particular story is being written up elsewhere, in a fictionalised account based on the true story.

Travels in a Young Country is a kind of "director's cut" of material that isn't included in the other book. Writing it during the *Writers for Ukraine* week brought home how lucky I was to have experienced Ukraine at its best. When I first began travelling to Ukraine, Russian aggression was already raging in the east of the country. The current systematic destruction of that world and the horrors inflicted on the people in 2022 are heart-breaking.

If you enjoy reading this book, please consider making a

donation to one of the charities supporting Ukraine and its people. I've added a few suggestions at the rear of the book.

While every story in this book is true, I have changed the names of people to protect their privacy.

Michelle Lawson
Devon, England
March 2022

CHAPTER 1

A SHADOWY LAND BEYOND THE IRON CURTAIN

As a child, I had a doll called Olga. But Olga was never one of the toy box gang. An old-fashioned porcelain doll sent by my father's sister in the USSR, Olga belonged in a museum rather than the toy box. And I knew so little about the people who'd sent her; what I was brought up to think of as a left-behind Polish family, stranded the other side of the Iron Curtain. Shadowy relatives in black and white photographs, posing in fields, among trees or against timber houses that in England we'd call a shed. Poor Olga developed a spidery fracture across her porcelain head and from then onwards I referred to her as Baby Crackhead, a sad symbol of my father's exile from his homeland.

My parents sent parcels packed with items such as razors and denim jeans to his sister in the USSR. Photographs and letters would arrive back, my mother frowning at anything written in the Cyrillic alphabet, as if the words were infected with communism. But it was the time of the Cold War, sparking a not unreasonable fear that my father's dual nationality would make our lives difficult if it ever came to a full-blown conflict. No wonder Baby Crackhead could never be part of the gang. She was an outsider, a foreigner associated with Soviet Russia.

My mother had another reason to be wary of that dark land on the other side of the Iron Curtain. She wasn't my father's first wife. He'd been married before the war to a young "Polish" woman who'd died within a couple of years of the wedding. My mother mentioned this to me only once. My father never raised the topic.

Despite not having lived in what became post-war Poland, my father seemed to have contacts everywhere in that country. During the late 60s and early 70s, he drove us to Poland for holidays, visiting cities such as Gdańsk, Wrocław and Poznań and the mountain resorts of Zakopane and Karpacz. And every Thursday lunchtime, he would close his barber shop and head to the Polish Club in Birmingham to mingle among people with a shared language.

One time my father secretly obtained a visa to drive into the USSR to visit his sister. The British government advised him they couldn't guarantee the safety of a dual national. *You go at your own risk.* Sure enough, the KGB arrested him and never let him out of their sight, allowing him just a few hours to talk with his sister. Among the things he brought back was a stomach ulcer from the stress.

So I was brought up to see myself as "half-Polish" in a rather superficial way. I'm not proud of the simplistic understanding I had, back then, of how my Polish father ended up in the English West Midlands. I knew only that he'd lived in a former chunk of eastern Poland and had escaped to wartime England before Stalin turned eastern Poland into the Ukrainian Soviet Socialist Republic. It wasn't until I looked into the history of the region that I realised how ethnicity and nationality couldn't be simplified like that. My father wasn't even born in Poland; his village lay within Austria during the first year of World War 1, although the land had historic associations with Poland. After 1772, when Poland was partitioned and disappeared from the map, much of present-day Western Ukraine formed the eastern part of the Austro-Hungarian province of Galicia. The region was a cultural blend of Poles, Germans and Jews within a Ukrainian majority. Only in 2018 did I discover that one of those Ukrainians had been my grandmother. It was my grandfather's side that had the Polish roots.

Back then Ukrainians were often known as "Ruthenian", a German-derived term that acknowledged these specific East Slavic people were neither Polish nor Russian. *Ruthenian* and *Rusyn* are derived from Rus', a name that goes back to the ancient Eastern Slavic trading empire of Kyivan Rus'. When the Austro-Hungarian empire broke up at the end of World War 1, Western Ukraine, along with parts of Lithuania and Belarus, became the eastern borderlands, or *kresy*, of interwar Poland. In 1919, Poland's right to occupy these borderlands was granted as a protection against the Bolsheviks. Ukraine's dream of independence was gone, its interests dismissed in favour of its neighbours.

As the 20th century unfolded, the name Ukraine, meaning borderland, or *beside the land*, came into use, alongside the desire for an independent Ukrainian state. Despite having to wait until 1992 for independence, the roots of Ukrainian nationhood go back a long way.

Poland's sovereignty over Galicia was recognised on the condition it would guarantee equal treatment for all its citizens. The Ukrainians naturally wanted the use of Ukrainian language within government, and an independent Ukrainian university. These assurances were never honoured. Schools became Polish speaking, Ukrainian newspapers were censored, Orthodox churches were converted to Catholicism, and Ukrainians were barred from government jobs.

Resentment grew in some rural areas where Polish landowners were a majority. Outraged at being forced to use Polish language when dealing with government administration, Ukrainians set arson attacks against the landowning Poles. The retaliatory Polish "pacification" could be brutal.

In many villages such as my father's, however, the cultural blend was deep-rooted, with mixed marriages going back generations. My Ukrainian grandmother married a Polish man, and in such families the sons followed their father's ethnicity, while daughters followed the mother's. How strange to think, then, of my father growing up Polish, while his sister and her offspring were Ukrainian. In such households there would be two Christmas celebrations: the Polish Catholic Christmas in December followed by the Greek Catholic (Ukrainian Uniate) celebration in early January.

Growing up, I'd had no idea of this. There was no mention of Ukrainians or Ruthenians, and certainly not Austrians. Everything was either Polish or "Russian".

Poland was ripped apart in 1939. Stalin moved into its eastern borderlands as part of the 1939 Molotov-Ribbentrop pact with the Nazis, abolishing Polish laws, currency and churches. Property was confiscated for collectivisation. Everyone became a Soviet citizen, although people could record a different nationality. "Undesirables" were deported east, meaning that professionals, the "bourgeois", and many Poles, including those guilty by association, were uprooted by means of a lengthy and dangerous journey to Siberia. Many did not survive it.

My father Mikołaj was one who did. Arrested by the Soviets, he was deported to a USSR prison camp in Siberia. When the Nazi-Soviet pact broke down in 1941, and the Germans moved into Soviet-occupied Ukraine, the departing Soviets granted a so-called "amnesty" for the deported Poles, to allow them to form a Polish army under British command. Mikołaj joined thousands of other Poles on the dangerous odyssey through the USSR down to Persia (Iran) to join the Polish II Corps, also known as the Anders Army. Dispatched from Palestine to a branch of the Polish Armed Forces in Europe, he sailed past Cape Town and Rio de Janeiro to disembark in Scotland. A serious motorbike accident put him out of action and into hospital for a year. He married my mother in Newton Abbot, and she brought Mikołaj to the outskirts of Birmingham. There he became Michael, a naturalised citizen of the UK.

Some years after my father's death, as I sorted through photographs and letters, I finally understood the words on the backs of the photographs were not Russian at all. The language was Ukrainian. It shares elements of the Cyrillic alphabet with Russian, but is nevertheless a distinct language. That distinction was never pointed out when I was growing up. As a child, I'd assumed the Soviets had forbidden the writing of letters in Polish, allowing only Russian. It turned out the letters went back and forth in Ukrainian.

In 2016 the Syrian civil war forced millions of asylum seekers to pursue safety in Europe. As nationalist rhetoric became mainstream on the UK's vote to exit the European Union, the issues of borders and forced exile became visible through a more personal lens. Watching the harrowing footage of displaced Syrians, I thought about my father, also a displaced person, who was fortunate to be granted British nationality. But the difficulties hadn't ended there. Mikołaj was sacked from his first job as a barber in Devon because local men refused to cut hair alongside a foreigner. As stories of prejudice opened up a deeper realisation of what he must have gone through, I thought about those he'd left behind.

I gathered all the photographs that had arrived over the past six decades. Frustratingly, there were few clues to who these people were, although I had the name of a cousin – Larysa – and her village. One photograph showed Larysa sitting in the middle of a large family gathering, dated 1974, surrounded by young adults and older people. The girls wore miniskirts, and two young boys sported the *oseledets* or *chupryna* hairstyle, the head shaved but for a single lock – the "herring" – in the centre. The hairstyle was a cultural icon for the Cossacks, and later Ukrainians used it to distinguish themselves against Russians. Meanwhile, the Russian name for it – *khokhol* – was a derogatory term for Ukrainians. How did these two boys get away with that hairstyle in 1970s USSR?

A second photograph of a different family puzzled me. The boy and his father gave hesitant smiles as they stared at the camera, but the mother and two daughters looked apprehensive. I returned to it again and again. Who was this second family, and why did they send photographs to my father?

The oldest photograph of all showed my father as a baby on his mother's lap, flanked by his elder sister and her daughter. That photograph dated from World War 1, when the two husbands were away fighting. At times the frontline was so close that the family would have been able to hear the artillery as the Russians and the Central Powers pounded each other.

After decades of indifference to that side of my family, it was a shock to find myself obsessed by the gaps in our family narrative. This kind of preoccupation is what the philosopher Nicolas Abraham referred to as transgenerational haunting. According to Abraham, it's not the dead themselves who haunt us; they aren't real. We're haunted by what we don't know, the gaps left by a loved one when they concealed some part of their life. These unspoken facts are the phantoms that haunt us.

I wasn't alone in finding myself, in middle age, obsessed by the knowledge concealed within my father's memory. So many other offspring of deportees find themselves fixated in later life by the lives of forgotten others. Their monochrome faces become scored into our imaginations as we search for ways to trace them.

CHAPTER 2

BY TRAIN INTO EUROPE'S DARK CORNERS

When I booked the trains spanning four days of travel from London to Western Ukraine in 2018, I hadn't realised I'd be following the same route my father had driven us as a family in the late 1960s and early 1970s.

Back then, driving to Poland involved what my nervous mother referred to as "going behind the Iron Curtain" that divided the West from the communist East. Day after day I sat squashed on the back seat of what was sometimes the only car on the roads of East Germany and Poland. Every few seconds the car jolted as it bounced over the joins between the concrete blocks of East German motorways. Children and adults would surround us every time we parked, eager to see what we would pull out of the boot. I had the job of handing out oranges, tomatoes, Wrigley's chewing gum, and sweets from a Quality Street tin.

Some fifty years later, I decided to replicate that journey in search of the family my father had left behind. Only this time I'd keep going into Ukraine.

LONDON TO BERLIN

Laptops opened as the Eurostar rolled out of London; a mundane commute to work for some. The four young people opposite, looking at their watches and talking about the departure time from *St Pancreas*, were planning their weekend in the beer emporium of Bruges. For me, it was the first of eight stages that would end a week later in the city closest to my dad's village – the city of Ivano-Frankivsk, closed off by the Soviets until the early 1990s. There I'd be met by a Ukrainian tour guide who offered grassroots genealogical research. Taras had already emailed me in triumph, having discovered people who remembered my father in the village. But these people were not directly related to me. They were the family of his first wife. A Ukrainian, not Polish, family.

Berlin had been a trigger of high tension on our Cold War journeys, being the crossing-place from the safety of the West into the unreliable land behind the Iron Curtain. Anything could happen to us on the other side, as my mother kept reminding us. My father's dual nationality status made him vulnerable to the moods of whichever official happened to be on duty. And it was no less fraught on the return crossing, when anxiety once more infected the car. Would some minor infringement prevent us from driving back into freedom?

That didn't stop my mother complaining to the East German guards as they made our passage through West and East Berlin as tedious as possible. It must have been on the return journey when the guards at Checkpoint Charlie – the crossing point for foreigners on the 830 mile zonal border between East and West Germany – disturbed me from my sleep on the back seat. Everyone was ordered out of the car. Border guards, dressed like actors in a Sunday afternoon war movie, leaned in and removed the entire back seat, then wheeled mirrors beneath the chassis to check we hadn't concealed any fugitives. They had no idea that the cushions I guarded on the back seat were stuffed full with goods.

. . .

In 2018 Checkpoint Charlie was a pantomime of Cold War replication. Uniformed actors posed and leaped around a sign warning that you were about to leave the American Sector. Every shop catered for memory tourists. Twenty-eight years after Checkpoint Charlie closed, it presented an anaesthetised version of yesteryear for those who hadn't experienced living through such oppression. A young woman thrust her phone at me, requesting a photo as she posed, arm on hip, in front of a piece of the Berlin Wall. Other tourists queued to stand, grinning, between two other fragments of the wall, ticking their way through the listicle of things to do in Berlin.

At nearby Charlie's Beach, young adults sat on benches surrounded by swept sand, choosing from a menu of burgers, ice cream and cocktails. This part of the city had a different meaning for twenty-year-old Berliners compared with memory tourists like me. Yet the city does a good job of committing to memory the more shocking aspects of its history. A few steps away, the Topography of Terror displayed glass panels with sobering reminders of the methods the Nazis used to take power. From 1933, this was the site of the Secret State Police Office, a hub of interrogation and torture for political prisoners. In one photograph, a male stood on a stone fountain decorated with swastika insignia, flanked by SS officers. A placard wider than his young body hung around his neck, stating, "I am a traitor to the people." His treason? Casting a *no* vote in a 1933 referendum on whether Germany should withdraw from the League of Nations.

Traitors. Enemies of the People. Language used by the

Nazis, by the Soviets and by the British tabloids not so long ago.

I crossed the city to the Berlin Wall Memorial, a grassed expanse dotted with rusting pillars. It's not immediately obvious what you're here to see, until the sixty-metre-long sweep of graffitied wall comes into view, along with information boards and photographs fixed to the pillars. Here, surrounded by apartment blocks, there were no selfie sticks or souvenirs, just a silent scatter of people reading the boards beneath a watchtower whose walls were deep in shadow, while the lowering sun bathed everything around it in gold. Just another dark corner of a city coming to terms with its past.

BERLIN TO WARSAW AND KRAKÓW

It was a surprise to step back in time on a Polish Intercity to Warsaw. Everything was brown and angular; the folding tables were heavy and clumsy, and the worn seats brown mock-velvet. It was far from what I'd expected for a six-hour journey on an international train, but it suited the fact that I was being sped – or rather, trundled – further east. The conversations were in Polish, and shortly after Frankfurt an der Oder the train crossed the river and the station names became Polish – Słubice, Kunowice – and the houses more squat, their low grey corrugated roofs dulling the landscape compared with the red-tiled roofs of East Germany.

The forests continued through the window, with an occasional glimpse of the main road between Berlin and Poznań. A German couple sat opposite and offered a share of their biscuits as a drink trolley came past. The coffee was decent and I took out my purse to pay, but the trolley had gone. "It's free," said the Germans. "It's a concession to this being an international service. The Polish don't have the rail stock to put on a decent train every time, so they offer free drinks to make up for having to sit in a train like this."

An elderly Polish man in a baggy grey suit shuffled on, confused as he looked around for his allocated seat. Hearing us talking, he tried out his own rusty German to wish us well before he left the train at an isolated station. Mixing languages raises no eyebrows here.

Stepping out of Warsaw station, a gargantuan tower block overshadowed everything: *The Palace of Culture and Science in the Name of Joseph Stalin*. Completed in 1955, it would have been visible in 1969 when we drove through a city I remembered for its tall buildings and wide streets. Five concentric towers rose from a squat base with classical columns and sculptures. At 237 metres, it's the highest building in Poland and one of the highest in the European Union. Designed as a multifunction public space, the Palace had been Stalin's gift to the citizens of Warsaw.

Like other relics from the Soviet years, the Palace polarises locals. Some would like to see it demolished. Some tolerate it but apply subversive nicknames, such as *Stalin's Dick*. Others view it as a symbol of Warsaw's phoenix-like rise from the post-war ashes. Whatever did the city's bombed-out inhabitants think of it at the time?

Modern glass skyscrapers came into view and the Palace took on a defiance as it faced the contemporary landscape of global blandness. Turn your back on Stalin's Palace, and you could be waiting to cross a road in Manchester or Birmingham to get to Caffe Nero, Vue Cinema or Pizza Hut. It was a relief to leave the faceless chains and walk beneath the reconstructed merchant houses of Rynok Square. Warsaw Old Town is now a UNESCO World Heritage Site, despite being rebuilt in a manner that wasn't entirely faithful to the original. Pristine and aesthetically pleasing, its walls moved through shades of terracotta, orange and pink to sage.

Yet, hard as I tried, I couldn't fully appreciate it. The Old Town's original function, and its link to the past, were absent, wiped out in the bombardment of 1944. Tonight, booming with music as young men sold glow sticks to tourists lifting their phones to capture the street entertainers, it was a place to walk through, rather than linger.

Dusk began to obscure the frescos reproduced on the walls enclosing the narrow streets of Warsaw Old Town. It felt churlish to complain about the lack of authenticity when the reconstruction had done such a decent job. But was it too easy to experience cities like this on a surface level, without acknowledging what lay beneath these streets? Perhaps some cities have too many buried memories.

It was 6pm in Kraków and bars were already booming music into the street. More than one screened a football match across the length of a back wall. Middle-aged men wearing English team shirts stood in clusters, munching kebabs and looking around for the next bar, while weekend couples leaned between tables to compare notes on sightseeing.

"We're doing Auschwitz tomorrow."

"We did it yesterday. It makes you think."

I hoped the understatement was a consequence of being lost for words. Auschwitz, one of Kraków's must-sees, is now an essential add-on, a bit of culture bolted onto a stag weekend.

With its mock Tube logo and a menu offering English breakfasts and fish and chips, the *Little Britain* bar stared out into Kraków's historic market square. According to TripAdvisor, customers like the reasonable prices, the English staff and the fact that the fish and chips are unaccompanied by grease. Elsewhere were the familiar logos of Costas and Starbucks. More than once I jumped as a cyclist balancing an Uber delivery box cut across me on the cobbles.

The frescoed stairway of my guest house raised my spirits, so it was disconcerting to see packaged earplugs placed on the bedside table. I'd just drifted off to sleep when the shrieking "Pub Krawl" stumbled into the bar opposite.

KRAKÓW TO L'VIV

The wide-gauge Ukrainian train bound for L'viv squealed to a halt at the border. With wide windows, television screens, Wi-Fi and spacious double and triple seats, this Ukrainian train was the most comfortable so far. A bargain to Western travellers, the train was an expensive luxury to many Ukrainians, who stuck to the buses.

Ukrainian border guards in camouflage jumpsuits vaulted into the carriage to demand passports and inspect baggage. One stood in front of me, her flinty eyes appraising me as she took my passport. "Do you have family here?"

"Maybe."

"Maybe!" she repeated, with a laugh, although it was a kindly one, as she stamped the passport and handed it back. Borders made me anxious, no doubt a leftover from those earlier trips behind the Iron Curtain. I needed to pull myself together. I was welcome here, unlike my father, whose one and only return culminated in a long night in the company of charmless KGB officers.

Once again, the landscape changed after crossing the border, and the stations, all tiny and deserted, had names painted in Cyrillic lettering. The lines of tall pine and birch were replaced by mixed woodland interspersed with open plots where a single chained cow grazed. Onion domes broke the skyline here and there. In Western Ukraine most churches are Uniate, the name formed from the union between the Roman Catholic church and the Ruthenian Orthodox. It's also known as Greek Catholic, a name that has little to do with anything Greek but distinguishes it from the Roman Catholic version. In my father's time, the Greek Catholic Church served the Ruthenian community, while the Roman Catholic Church, associated with the Habsburg empire, served the Poles. As his village had no Polish church to serve the tiny Polish minority, he must have gone to the Ukrainian church with his Ukrainian mother and sister.

All of that was outlawed when the Soviets made Western Ukraine part of the USSR. The Soviets allowed only the Moscow Patriarchal Orthodox Church. Other churches were put to secular use, sometimes as storage, sometimes as a cinema. The church in my father's village became a museum of atheism.

The landscape became more urban as Soviet-era blocks rose alongside swanky newer apartments, and the train pulled into L'viv's monumental Art Nouveau railway station. As I left the station I experienced a mild culture shock, although it was also thrilling to look back at the enormous dome of the station. Taking on a pale red cast from the lowering sun, the name Львів symbolised how far east I had travelled.

CHAPTER 3

LVIV'S QUIRKY MEMORY TOURISM

BACK IN 1914, L'viv was Lemberg, a diverse Austro-Hungarian city populated by Poles, Austrians and Jews, as well as Ruthenians/Ukrainians. At the end of World War 1, the Poles and the Ukrainians fought on the streets of Lemberg as the latter declared a new country: the West Ukrainian People's Republic. But that independence was tragically short-lived. Lemberg became Polish Lwów for a couple of decades before the city endured a tug-of-war status between Germans and Soviets in World War 2. The following decades of Sovietisation brought yet another name to the city – Russian Lvov – that ended in 1991 when Ukraine became independent, and the city became L'viv.

In 2018 L'viv was undergoing a rapid discovery by tourists. That year more than two million visited the city, and Ryanair were about to start flying in from London. I'd heard the city referred to as 'the new Prague', reducing it to a city of weekend visits: affordable beer, splendid architecture and souvenir shops. It's an understandable description of a city that escaped the bombs of World War 2. Yet although the city's buildings survived, the population mix did not, a fact often concealed beneath L'viv's complex strata of history and memory. Layers of what was lost lie beneath what was left behind, sometimes forgotten but not entirely erased. More than anything, L'viv is a city of absences, having experienced some dark years of occupation that profoundly changed its character.

The Nazi and Soviet regimes took no time to destroy the multicultural character of Lemberg/Lwów that had survived for centuries. The Poles themselves, who made up around half of the interwar population, are long gone, killed or deported.

All told, around 80 percent of the city's pre-war dwellers disappeared, including the Jewish residents who'd made up a third of Lwów's inhabitants. From the safety of

1946 New York, the Polish poet Józef Wittlin, a former inhabitant of the city, imagined the ghostly footsteps of its former dwellers, shuffling along the pavements of post-war Soviet Lvov as their places were filled by Ukrainians from elsewhere, particularly those who'd inhabited south-east Poland, as well as other Slavic peoples from the Soviet Union. Few of those living here today are descendants of L'viv's pre-war occupants.

The hill that sloped down from the station was thick with toxic fumes erupting from small yellow buses packed with standing passengers. I kept my eyes on the crooked pavements, noting the roads weren't much better. The towers and spires of L'viv's old town remained concealed behind the tall buildings that lined the hill.

And yet a thrill rose in me as I walked down the hill into a city that felt both alien and comforting. Stepping off the train, after days spent travelling eastwards, I was finally in a landscape where the language was the one on the backs of the old photographs. The boxy Ladas and the women in headscarves brought my senses closer to an understanding of where I was. And although present-day Ukraine is dislocated from the interwar Poland of my father's memory, that didn't make it irrelevant. I was convinced I had family here somewhere. Despite having no tangible link to L'viv, I sensed that those gaps in my family history, those cracks within my own sense of who I was and where I was from, were a little closer to getting filled.

Neo-Renaissance columns, a vaulted ceiling and a magnificent dual staircase overshadowed the tiny reception desk of L'viv's historic George Hotel. Climbing the sweeping stairways was like heading up to an Austro-Hungarian imperial banquet. That feeling evaporated on entering the Superior room with its grubby carpet and sunken mattress. In its time, the oldest of the city's hotels had been a meeting place for L'viv intellectuals, bohemians, political and military elite. Sartre, Strauss, and Yuri Gagarin were among its illustrious guests. *The George Times*, an A3 brown paper publication left on the breakfast tables, described the hotel as a place for writers who take inspiration from the setting. The public areas certainly imbued a sense of imperial Lemberg, and the George is deservedly popular, but the six-inch gap between the "double glazing" failed to diminish the rumble of wheels over the cobbles throughout the night.

Walking around L'viv's central Rynok Square, one hears the painstaking tap-tap-tap chipping away at centuries of grime behind scaffolded facades. The city's fusion of architectural styles has earned its inclusion in UNESCO's World Heritage list, beginning with physical reminders of Lemberg in the opera house and its parks. L'viv's fame as a coffee centre is another Austrian legacy, celebrated in an annual festival and the city's themed cafes. In one of the cafes you can descend the stairs to a "coffee mine", where you're handed a helmet to walk safely through the tunnel, all disbelief suspended as you walk past heaps of freshly-mined coffee beans.

Until very recently, L'viv's inhabitants seemed unwilling to acknowledge the city's non-Ukrainian heritage, as Philippe Sands noted in *East West Street*. Not so long ago, there was little to commemorate, or even acknowledge, the former existence of L'viv's ghetto and concentration camp. Visitors with a personal interest must have wondered why all traces of the city's Jewish heritage had been annihilated along with the people themselves. But finally, L'viv is coming to terms with its lost inhabitants. A new memorial garden stood close to the railway "Bridge of Death" on the site of the old ghetto entrance. Nearby was Janowska, a horribly multifunctional Nazi camp for the Jews. Janowska acted as a transit hub to other concentration camps, as well as offering a source of Jewish slave labour for local factories. It was also, of course, a final destination in itself.

What to make, then, of the Galician Jewish restaurant *At the Golden Rose*, where the cost of the dishes depends on the customer's bargaining skills? Standing right next to the ruins of L'viv's former Golden Rose Synagogue, the restaurant employs staff wearing mock Jewish headgear and sidelocks. Not surprisingly, its reception has been mixed, and no one I spoke with approved of it. But as long as enough customers like it, it seems to matter little if others find it objectionable. And plenty do like it, according to the rating on TripAdvisor, where customers leave reviews evaluating it as *funny* and *interesting*.

L'viv's young entrepreneurs make the most of history's commercial value with these bizarre restaurants, and people seem happy to go along with consumer nostalgia. Commemoration on a superficial level allows visitors to appreciate the past by dipping their toes into it while they eat a quirky meal, leaving more complex and difficult questions at a distance. At the very least, how can people not consider how such a place might cause offence and even pain in a city where some 110,000 of the population were murdered for being Jewish?

Awareness of the commercial value of Old Poland is also growing. Poles have never forgotten how this city was theirs for a time. To many Poles, L'viv remains Lwów, a city of the Second Polish Republic, and to this end, the Polish government has invested towards aspects of its restoration. Vestiges of Polish Lwów linger in its churches and in the Polish language "ghost signs" that are coming to light beneath chipped-away paint and plaster. Most of L'viv's walking tour guides draw attention to this phenomenon. Dating mostly from the interwar period of Polish Lwów, these signs in Polish were covered up by the Soviets, for whom the Poles were an inconvenient reminder of the city's pre-USSR days. Now more of these signs are being renovated as the city moves towards a more open remembrance of its multicultural heritage.

Slowly, the remembrance void is being filled. L'viv nowadays is a homecoming destination for memory tourists of many nationalities. Visitors reversing the exile of their ancestors are the true descendants of the city.

I latched onto a city walking tour and Luba, the guide, led us into a small bar. "Tourists don't bother to come in here," she said. Almost everyone on the walking tour was in L'viv for an IT conference. Luba nodded. "L'viv is booming with its IT services, and a lot of work is outsourced to us. That sector has the best salaries. But other professions pay well here now. One of the best salaries at the moment is that of a tractor driver, a thousand dollars a month!"

After the tour ended, I walked up towards Castle Hill, hoping the crowds would thin out. Instead, I found myself fighting for space where people spilled down the coach steps and onto the pavements. L'viv was close to being a victim of its own splendour.

A few metres away rose the glass balconies of a brand-new monument to the Heavenly Hundred, the people killed by security forces during the Maidan protests. Ukraine's Euromaidan revolution had been triggered by President Yanukovych rolling back an agreement for tighter association with Europe. Putin viewed that association as a betrayal; in his eyes, Ukraine was a post-Soviet client state of Russia that had no business looking westwards. Under pressure, Yanukovych pulled out of the European association at the last minute, to the disgust of many Ukrainians who called on their president to resign. The resulting protests lasted for months, with support from most of Ukrainian society: students, educated liberals, nationalists, business owners and factory workers, all outraged at the corruption, the oligarchic system and the broken promises of Yanukovych's Russia-backed government. When the regime collapsed in 2014, Yanukovych fled to Russia, prompting Putin to take Crimea and spark the war in Donbas.

Level with the city's domes and towers, I looked down at the snaking lines of weekend visitors, enjoying a peaceful city far from the war in the east as they queued for cherry vodka shots and restaurant "experiences", donated to street touts in exchange for a tiny blue and yellow flag, and drank beer next to cardboard cut-outs of Obama in the Pravda Beer Theatre. No less a borderland today than it was during the tugs-of-war of the past, L'viv is sufficiently different to be exotic. At the same time, the city provides comforting reminders of Central Europe.

. . .

The following day, I met up with Xenia, an academic who'd been teaching me Ukrainian language lessons via Skype. I'd arranged a couple of face-to-face sessions with her in L'viv to get me into the swing of conversation. We sat down for coffee outside the town hall, where I asked about Ukrainian attitudes towards closer integration with Europe.

"I want to have closer links with Europe, yes. Around a million Ukrainians work in Europe now. We do a lot of trade with the EU, too. You must have noticed how you can buy anything here these days." I nodded. "But I wonder whether joining the EU would be the best way forward," said Xenia. "On the one hand, Ukraine could maintain its national ideals and independence within the EU, just like Poland. But Ukraine is still a developing country. It might be better to make the changes internally, make reforms from within Ukraine, as a response to our specific needs, rather than change them to suit the EU's rules."

It was similar to some of the more reasoned arguments I'd heard for Brexit, although of course the context was very different. Britain had grown and developed over decades with Europe; Ukraine was a fledgling country, still finding its way. And yet both contexts share a fundamental problem: electing a government that can be trusted to introduce or replace regulations that have people's interests at heart, rather than profit.

Xenia also distrusted the West as a safety net. "On Ukraine's independence we gave up our nuclear weapons and our borders were guaranteed protection, but look what happened in 2014, when Russia invaded in the east!

You can't trust guarantees any more. And is Europe really that perfect place? From what I've seen, Europeans work too hard." She gestured at the people standing at the cherry vodka stand opposite. "Here, I think, we have a better life."

This wasn't just the imagination of someone who'd never left their country. Xenia had travelled extensively in Europe. Everywhere except the UK. "Other countries allow Ukrainians to visit without a visa for up to three months. We made it clear during the Maidan revolution that we feel European, so Europe appreciates that and makes us welcome. And visa-free travel allows Ukrainians to fill the gaps left by the Poles and others, when they go to work in other richer countries. But the visa concession doesn't apply to Britain. That's why I haven't ever visited your country."

Looking around L'viv's Rynok Square, the most obvious difference between L'viv and the cities of England was the lack of homeless people sitting in doorways. Xenia explained it as a consequence of the former communist policy.

"Before independence, all property belonged to the state. Post 1991, the government voted in a socialist solution, where you automatically became the owner, or part-owner, of the property you were living in. Nowadays, people only rent if they move to a town or city for work." People also could apply for a subsidy towards utilities that cost more than 15 percent of their income.

Xenia handed me a bunch of leaflets. Which of the city's experiences would I like to visit? I shook my head as I flicked through them until my finger traced a grubby-looking Union flag on the cover of one. *British Club L'viv.* "I'd like to see this place."

We climbed the stairs to a reception desk flanked by a portrait of Winston Churchill. To the left draped a Union flag, its wooden dowel slotted through elaborate floral metalwork. Around the corner hung a bored-looking Princess Diana in shiny pink; next to her strolled Prince Philip along a lake edge. L'viv's British Club was founded by a British man with Ukrainian heritage. The cost of a stay here was at the higher end for L'viv.

Every Thursday afternoon, my father had attended the Polish Club in Birmingham to eat *bigos* and *pierogi* among fellow Polish exiles. I'd assumed this was a similar kind of place for British immigrants working in L'viv, providing familiarity for the homesick. But I saw little more than a stereotype of Britain rooted in the romance of nostalgia; a version dislocated from the reality experienced by most Britons. The Club's portraits and heavy furniture were more representative of the average British stately home. Even the Union flag of the Club's logo was aged with artful discolouration, an attempt to hark back to the past. Who, exactly, stayed here?

"Our guests are mostly Polish," admitted the receptionist.

Now I understood. The British Club broadened the range of memory tourism options in L'viv, offering an outdated version of Britain that foreign tourists like to see.

CHAPTER 4
FACES COME TO LIFE

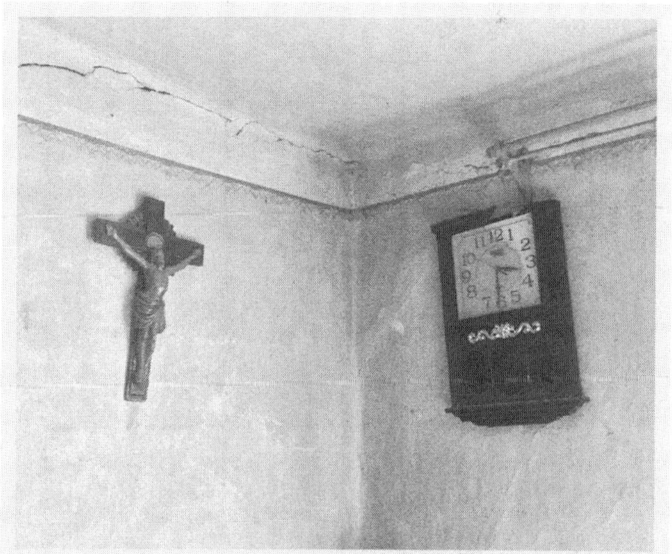

TARAS, driving me south from Ivano-Frankivsk, steered his shiny new Škoda around a large sunken area that took up the entire width of our side of the road. Taras was the tour guide and amateur genealogist I'd paid to go into my father's village and look for my cousins. Instead, he'd discovered people I'd never dreamed existed: the family of the Ukrainian girl my father married in the 1930s. Taras had filmed himself talking to these in-laws, and today he was driving me to meet them. The people seemed helpful in the films and they told stories about my father. But wasn't it odd going to visit the relatives of my father's first wife? He'd never even mentioned her to me. People back at home shook their heads at the thought of doing such a thing. Why would Ukrainian people be interested in the English daughter of a man who'd left seventy-six years ago?

Cranes broke the skyline alongside new "comfort" apartments that emphasised the patched-up state of the Soviet-era blocks. Taras saw me looking. "Ukrainians go to Poland to earn money, because the Polish workers are in places like Britain. They come back here and use the money they earn to buy an apartment." He was pragmatic about the scheduled Ryanair route to L'viv. "We know there'll be loads of English people flying over for the cheap beer. But it's good for us Ukrainians. An opportunity for business."

Taras took a diversion to avoid the traffic in the town of Bohorodchany, where my father had worked for a Polish hairdresser during the 1930s. In my bag I had a book by writer Andrew Zalewski, who had researched his own family history in Bohorodchany. Zalewski wrote how the "remarkable harmony" of the 19th century gave way to conflict between Poles and Ukrainians between the wars; the very time my father had worked in the town. As we skirted the urban landscape, I wondered whether the growing conflict between the Poles and the Ukrainians had affected our family. Those events were a long time ago, and the two countries seemed supportive of each other these days, but after reading so much about the conflict I felt a little nervous heading for a Ukrainian village from where my Polish father had been deported in 1940. Would there be any resentment towards me?

The car turned onto an unsurfaced track and Taras drove even more slowly as we skirted individual houses guarded by enormous gates decorated with curving and twisting metalwork. One gate was flanked with panels of hammered metal, the surface split with methodical mock rips "fixed" with oversized staples. The single-story houses behind the gates were modest in comparison. Soon the golden lozenges of the church dome came into view.

The car pulled up outside a house, and a nervous-looking woman came out. Taras introduced me to Daryna, who was the wife of Andriy, my father's nephew-in-law. Andriy was at work, but Daryna led me, an English stranger, into her garden, where hundreds of pumpkins lay on the grass. That was a startling sight, but nothing compared to what lay behind: the old house built in 1934 where my father had lived with his wife and her family. Deep red wood panels skirted walls the colour of the sky, topped by a rust-laden metal sheet roof. The windows of the front porch had elaborate fretwork, and ragged curtains hung in most of them, while those without glass were stuffed with blocks of hay.

Taras explained that he was going to collect Olena, the mother of Daryna's husband Andriy. He gestured towards the open doorway. "You're free to go in, these people don't care what you do." The main room was filled with bundles of old clothes and building materials. A clock hung in the corner, the fingers frozen at three-thirty. In another corner was an ancient cooking range, brown ceramic tiles gleaming through the dust mites.

What would my father have seen, looking out from the window with its drooping net curtain? Possibly the well, with its narrow blue slats; maybe racks of sliced apple similar to those drying in the sun. A world reduced to memories, kept alive in occasional letters, photographs and one frightening visit.

Olena walked down the path, leaning heavily on a stick. Olena was the widow of Mihail, the younger brother of the girl my father had married in the 1930s. We stood in front of the well and I pulled out the photographs. One by one she shook her head at each photograph. "Other people."

I handed her the photo of the big family gathering, the people who I thought were my cousins. "What about this photo?"

More head-shaking. "Other people. A man with sixteen children." Did I have sixteen cousins? She didn't know.

I handed Olena the photo of the second, smaller family, and the reaction was instant. "My Mihail!" she cried, "and me, and my children, Yuliya, Andriy and Katya!"

A breakthrough at last. Olena was the mother in the photo that had puzzled me, the family of five. My father's *in-laws.* They not only knew who he was, but they had kept in touch, sending him photos. The awkwardness I'd felt, an English stranger, on walking into their garden disappeared.

Everyone was smiling now. Daryna invited me into the house for lunch.

I passed around small gifts from home, bland tourist souvenirs I'd chosen to give to people I knew nothing about. Daryna's grandchildren looked puzzled as they opened boxes of clotted cream fudge and flicked through the postcards of North Devon. Daryna and Olena accepted the tea towels illustrated with Devon tourist traps.

The table was laid with beetroot, mushrooms, beans and a bottle of clear liquid that Daryna poured into shot glasses. *Horilka* (or *Horivka*) is a generic term for alcohol distilled from grain such as wheat or rye, such as vodka. As Taras introduced this one as moonshine, I guessed we were downing shots of *samohon*, which translates as "self-distilled".

Taras translated Daryna's questions. "She asks how big is your house and your land, and if you have animals like a cow or a pig."

I tried to describe our small, terraced house with its steep and narrow garden that was originally built as a small-holding croft. "No one in the terrace keeps animals like that now."

Daryna nodded slowly, her eyes weighing me up. "I think you eat fast food,' she said.

"They have photographs of you too," said Taras, "that your father sent. They knew he had two daughters."

I stared at Daryna and she nodded back. All the time, this other family had been exchanging letters and photographs with my father. He was little more than a story to them, although Olena had spoken briefly to him when he made that dangerous journey here in the early 1970s.

She'd gone up the hill as a proxy for her husband, whom the KGB had forbidden to talk to my father, because Mihail had been a teenage mediator for the Ukrainian partisans. Along with thousands of other nationalists, he'd been deported to Siberia, released on the thaw after Stalin's death.

I leaned across to Taras and asked if we could visit the churchyard, where I could look for relatives.

"Of course." He spoke with Daryna, who nodded. "She'll take you up to the cemetery."

Taras drove us past the church, where the entire population of the village, wearing traditional embroidered *vyshyvanka* shirts, were pouring out of the doors after a service. Heads stared at the shiny new vehicle driven by a young man in dark sunglasses. I smiled through the window, warmed by a sense of belonging, however tenuous it was.

Daryna led me up to where the dead lay in neat rows across the hillside. Weathered photographs imposed onto oval frames stared out from headstones. I stopped to look into each face while Daryna continued walking. Soon she called out in triumph. "Larysa!"

The face superimposed onto the headstone was unmistakable; features that were older but more at peace than the woman in the centre of the family gathering. In the 1974 photograph, surrounded by her husband and all those children, my cousin's face imparted resignation, a difficult life endured. On the headstone, however, the smile was faint as she dared to acknowledge the peace she'd found in her later years.

A bittersweet moment. My father would have been sixteen when his great-niece was born. She would have been a small child at his wedding. If only I'd begun my search seven or eight years earlier, I'd have been able to meet Larysa.

But there was something else. Larysa's headstone was grander than anything around it and, unlike some of the others, there were no weeds growing through. Someone kept it tidy. Someone had placed a couple of red candles in glass jars. Someone close to Larysa – perhaps one of the sixteen children – was around to tend her grave.

CHAPTER 5

IN KOLOMIYA WITH A GIANT EGG

After visiting my father's village I took a bus to Kolomiya, a gateway to the Carpathian Mountains. My hotel overlooked one of two celebrated museums, the clue being an enormous concrete egg below my balcony. Painted yellow, orange and red, the egg was a world-famous museum of decorated *pysanky* eggs. Egg painting has been practised in this part of the world for thousands of years, and as a child, I'd played with carved and painted wooden versions that my father brought back from his trips to Poland.

The hotel receptionist seemed flummoxed by my printed reservation, but she was happy enough for me to walk behind the counter and point it out on the computer screen.

"Is there a tourist office?" I asked.

"*Ny*."

I'd come to Kolomiya because my guidebook claimed it was a good base for getting out into the Carpathians. But what the Lonely Planet really meant was that Kolomiya was a good base if you happen to stay in one of two guest houses where the owners will arrange everything for you, providing transport and acting as hiking guides. Over the following days I discovered how the relatively low Carpathians were not easily accessible without a lot of organising. They were barely even visible from Kolomiya.

A balcony overlooking a painted concrete egg was poor compensation for a hike in the Carpathians. On the other hand, it seemed a shame to spend three days overlooking this bizarre museum without entering it. I climbed the steps into the oval interior, greeting the huddle of female staff doing little but laughing together, and wandered around the display cases lining the gently curving walls of the egg. Once I'd come full oval, I exited the egg, eyes blurred from the intricacy but no wiser as to what each loop and twist represented.

The other famous museum celebrated the Hutsul people, an ethnic Carpathian group that stretches across national borders. Of Slavic origin, they sometimes distinguish themselves with the term Rusyn rather than that of Ukrainian/Ruthenian.

This time the three female staff looked up from their television and greeted me as I entered the Hutsul museum. One of them got to her feet and followed me up the curving stone staircase with its stained-glass windows, pressing icons on a screen to play the sounds of traditional *duda* bagpipes and the long wooden *trembita* pipe, a "telephone of the mountains" used to call across the Carpathians.

In Kolomiya's market, stalls sold traditional embroidered Ukrainian shirts known as *vyshyvanka*. These shirts are worn by men and women as symbols of Ukrainian unity. In earlier times the designs formed part of a language of nature, protecting from evil and symbolising loyalty between couples. Nowadays they're worn at weddings and on religious and national holidays, reinforcing a sense of Ukrainian identity. Would I be guilty of cultural appropriation if I bought one? My father brought Polish costumes back from his visits when I was a child, and I'd worn them for school photographs. Knowing now that my father's roots were as much Ukrainian as Polish, it was surely acceptable to acknowledge my own Ukrainian heritage with a traditional shirt. The stallholder nodded approvingly as I chose a *vyshyvanka* embroidered with blue and gold, two colours that embellish so much of Ukraine.

Three circuits of Kolomiya revealed little more than shops, churches and the market. Kolomiya, the Gateway to the Carpathians, appeared to have no visitor services. It did, however, have a bar called The London Underground.

In a square with elegant Austro-Hungarian architecture, a London Tube icon blazed out with the word "pub" printed across the centre. The same cultural icon I'd seen at Little Britain in Kraków, it was far more astonishing here, in a Ukrainian town that appeared to have no other English-speaking tourists. I walked down the steps into a bar where the walls were pinned with European football scarves.

I asked the barman what had been puzzling me. "Why The London Underground, here in Kolomiya?"

"Because London is full of pubs. Here we have just one, so it's special for us."

"*Us* meaning the locals?"

He nodded. "And some of the locals have worked in Britain."

So it was the opposite of the bar in Kraków. There, Little Britain was an antidote to Polish voices and unintelligible menus. That bar provided tourists with a breathing space from too much foreignness. Order in English and you'll know what you're getting; even better, the fish and chips are served without our national grease. The London Underground, on the other hand, provided exoticism for

Ukrainians who appreciated feeling they were part of Europe.

Walking back to the hotel, the sky suddenly darkened to pewter and let loose heavy drops of rain. As I ran, my eye was caught by a circle of white skin showing through the worn heel of a sock. A man lay fast asleep on one of the town's benches; he'd taken the precaution of placing his boots beneath the bench. When he awoke, he'd have nice, dry boots for his wet feet.

On my third day in Kolomiya, I took the bus to Yaremche, a tourist resort in the Carpathians. I'd considered staying there rather than Kolomiya, but its description of a main road with a giant souvenir market clustered around a moderate waterfall had underwhelmed me, compared with a real town like Kolomiya. After a couple of days wandering around Kolomiya's museums and market, Yaremche was beginning to sound attractive.

The ancient buses lined up were smaller than their European counterparts. It was as if they'd been cut in half, unwilling to seat no more than twenty or so. They idled, belching black fumes, apart from the single newer model that was being bump-started.

Ukrainian bus stations are patrolled by a woman who walks around making sure that passengers have a ticket and can locate their bus. Kolomiya's bus lady pointed me in the direction of the bus to Yaremche and I climbed the steps into a dark interior. Thin blue curtains, damp with condensation, blocked out light from the grimy windows. The bus started up with a squeal of the fan belt that drowned out the radio music, and the bus lurched across potholes the size of garden ponds.

The bus trundled past crafts piled up to sell at the roadside: willow pannier baskets laid in a circle, twig brooms leaning into a tepee shape. Bridge railings were painted in Ukraine's national colours of yellow and blue, symbolising the fields of grain meeting the sky. The nation must have burst forth in a mania of painting when Ukraine became independent, although the flag itself had been around for a hundred years or so.

After half an hour, the road began to climb and the view opened out to moorland. Then came the wooded foothills of the Carpathians, with low-slumbering mountains visible as silhouettes from time to time.

At Yaremche, I followed a thin line of stragglers along the main road running parallel to the River Prut, past a couple of decaying and incomplete concrete hotels. A woman thrust a leaflet at me, and I stopped to look at the tours on offer.

"English?"

"*Ny*," she said with a scowl, and snatched back the leaflet.

A few yards further, the same happened. This time I kept the leaflet. The first tour was a trip back to where I'd come from: the Pysanky Egg Museum. There were guided walks to waterfalls, excursions to castles further afield, and even a trip to L'viv. I passed another three women holding the same leaflets by the roadside. But my tentative question about whether English was spoken was always met with a curt "*ny*". They weren't going to waste their time with me.

Yaremche's famed souvenir market snaked up a slope

adjacent to the River Prut. Stall after stall sold the same items: Ukrainian embroidered *vyshyvanka* shirts, uncomfortably thick knitted socks and mass-produced versions of the Hutsul woollen waistcoat. The rain and the watchful proprietors gazing out from the stalls cast a bleakness over the enterprise. On one stall I recognised stringed bead necklaces similar to those worn by my aunt in the photograph from over a hundred years ago. The seller came over. "Where you from? America, Canada?"

"England."

He furrowed his eyebrows. "England . . . The town England?"

What might he recognise? "The town London," I said. Accuracy wasn't important.

"Ah," he said with a nod. "London."

The stall next door sold knitted versions of the traditional embroidered shirts, and I picked out one of the plainer ones to hold against me. The two women giggled and pointed to a different, more elaborate style, with pink rather than blue. I recognised the word *cholovik*, and realised I'd picked up the male version. But I preferred its plainness, although it gave off a strong smell of root vegetables. The women giggled again as I handed over the notes. It would need a good soak before I wore it.

CHAPTER 6

THE NUMBER 9 TRAM: L'VIV IN DECEMBER

CLANKING and dinging as they glide along the rails, shrieking and slanting as they negotiate corners, L'viv's trams criss-cross the city along nine routes. Wrapped up against the Ukrainian December, clutching a handful of tram tickets, I boarded the number 7 tram to L'viv's most famous cemetery. Spreading across the wooded hillside, Lychakiv's forty-two acres are more like an unconventional open-air museum where you stroll around the resting ground of politicians, the wealthy and the celebrated. Austrian Lemberg, Polish Lwów, Soviet Lvov and Ukrainian L'viv; all were there, in the names of the dead.

The paths winding up the hills were paved with the remains of crushed stone from an earlier policy to recycle the headstones of untended graves. The path led through graves decorated with red candle jars, the dead placed intimately close to their neighbours, but further up the hillsides, the graves thinned out into sporadic crooked markers among stubborn clumps of snow. One grave from the Soviet years held a modern life-sized sculpture of a naked woman sitting at the edge of the plinth. In contrast nearby stood a small and ghostly white figure, her eyes fixed in dread at something over my shoulder. Surrounded by brittle leaves and unrestrained ivy, a few stubborn flakes of blue clung to her dress, the stalk of a plastic orange flower threaded through the gap in her fingers.

Lower down were the adjacent military cemeteries of the Ukrainian – Polish war of 1918-19. Despite the age of the remains, the cemeteries opened only in 2005, after what we might call a war of memory; a conflict between differing versions of events, depending on whoever was in charge at the time.

A sea of small white crosses spread along the Polish cemetery. But the war was not fought against invaders. The Polish Eaglets, fighting for control of Lwów after the collapse of the Austrian Empire, battled against the indigenous Ukrainians. Friend pitched against friend, the two sides sometimes fraternising during ceasefires, adding poignancy to the fact that the "Defenders of Lwów" were little more than children when they sacrificed their lives. Back then, the victorious Poles buried the Ukrainian defenders more modestly elsewhere. The divide deepened further with the use of inflammatory language by Polish media, celebrating the victory of the Poles over *murderous Ukrainian savages.*

When Ukraine became independent, the Polish and Ukrainian authorities set to work to repair the cemetery after decades of Soviet neglect. The Poles restored what the Soviets had turned into a truck depot into that sea of white and red crosses. The Ukrainians, beginning from scratch, moved their graves here and crowned their cemetery with a granite obelisk topped by the archangel Michael. Despite the archangel turning his back on the Poles, the two nations claimed solidarity with each other at the cemetery's opening in 2005.

Many of the Ukrainian crosses bore the initials OUN and UPA. OUN was the Organisation of Ukrainian Nationalists, a movement formed in 1929 towards an independent state of Ukraine. In June 1941, when the Nazis captured L'viv from the Soviets, OUN members initially welcomed the German invaders, seeing them as allies against the Polish oppressors here and the Soviet repressors in the eastern lands. The enemy of my enemy is my friend, as it were.

Seemingly liberated at last, Western Ukraine proclaimed its independence and the Ukrainians set about establishing a regional government. But Hitler was having none of it. Contemptuous of the Slavic race, he ordered Himmler to eliminate the fledgling Ukrainian State Administration.

Some refer to this as "collaboration", tainting the entire Ukrainian nationalist movement with the short-lived association with the Nazi occupiers. Others I spoke with shook their heads at that word. "It was a cooperation rooted in hope of independence," a young man told me in L'viv. "The Nazis played the nationalists to serve their own interests. They wanted Ukraine for its space and food-growing potential. With hindsight, it's clear they would never have supported an independent Ukrainian state."

By the end of 1942, the OUN partisans went underground and formed their own military organisation, the UPA partisan (or insurgent) army. As the Germans retreated, the partisans turned their efforts to fighting the returning Soviets, a struggle that continued well after the end of the war. The Russians tried to control the partisans by deporting as many as they could arrest, along with their families, as a way to weaken their support and deter others from joining. Over six days in October 1947, 78,000 people were deported from Western Ukraine to Siberia: partisans, their wives, sons and daughters. The following year I discovered that one of them had been my cousin, whose "crime" was being married to a man conscripted into the partisan army. The Soviets never allowed her to return home.

Further along was a section of more recent graves: Ukrainian defenders killed by the current war in the east.

Shiny new granite crosses bore the letters OUN and UPA, rooting Ukraine's struggle for independence within its past. The partisans were far from relegated to history.

In a bid to escape the past, I headed to Rynok Square for a contemporary view of the city's rooftops. The ticket seller at L'viv's town hall tower tried to tell me something but shook her head with irritation at my lack of comprehension, taking my money with a shrug. After more than 400 twisting narrow steps, I emerged onto the tower's observation platform above the domes and spires of the Austrian Empire. From up here, L'viv was a toy town, its grand terraces in shades of yellow, topped with the bright greens and deep rusts of their roofs, muted through patches of light snow. A view previously forbidden to Westerners; the paranoid Soviets feared the panorama was too useful for plotting an attack.

Everyone jumped as a siren blasted out, its screech radiating from right here at the top of the tower. People moved around the platform, their hands pressed to their hats and hoods either side of their heads, mouths opening and closing soundlessly; the pain of assaulted eardrums tinged with humour at the absurdity. Abruptly, the horrible wailing ended, and a man emerged from a small shed in the centre of the platform. He smiled an apology, he was just servicing the city's warning siren, and people shuffled back to the edge to pose for photographs. Two minutes later, everyone jerked again as the din blasted through the air. Unbearable! It was only when I passed the ticket desk that I realised what the woman had been trying to warn me about.

My ears ringing, I leaped onto a tram without bothering to check where it was going. It trundled along the curves of the street, an ominous clunk striking through my seat as the tram cambered each bend and climbed uphill. Just like the city itself, L'viv's streets had changed their names according to whoever was in charge. In 1945, this street had carried the name of Josef Stalin. These days the street carries the name of Stepan Bandera, a nationalist symbol of the fight for Ukrainian independence.

I left the tram at Kropyvnyts'kyi Square, opposite a huge post-modern triumphal arch curving up towards the darkening sky. In front was a statue, although it wasn't one of the usual poets such as Taras Shevchenko or Ivan Franko. No, this man wearing a flapping coat over a suit and tie was in a different category of national hero.

The last rays of the sun caught the gold Cyrillic lettering of his name: Stepan Bandera. For some, that name symbolised Ukraine's fight for independence. For others, it threw a shadow tainted by fascism and bloody intimidation.

Born five years before my father in the same region, Bandera was educated at a time when it was officially forbidden to utter the term *Ukrainian*. For the interwar rulers of 'Eastern little Poland', the word *Ukrainian* was an unwelcome sign of political consciousness. As far as the Polish government was concerned, only *Ruthenian* could be used. This was a time when fascist ideals were developing elsewhere, inspiring nationalists such as Bandera, who viewed them as a logical way to get rid of Ukraine's Polish occupiers. In the 1930s, Bandera was involved in nationalistic assassination attempts on Polish ministers, which led to his imprisonment. The Nazis released him in 1939 and his ideals became more radical, splitting the OUN nationalists into two factions. OUN-B, named after Bandera, was the more radical side. In 1941, as the Soviets retreated from the Nazis, it was Bandera who declared an independent Ukraine. The Nazis wasted no time in sending Bandera to Sachsenhausen.

Bandera spent his later years in prison or in hiding until a Soviet agent assassinated him in 1959. As the street name and the statue suggest, Bandera is celebrated these days as an early fighter for Ukraine's independence. And after decades of Soviet repression, the government's decommunisation campaign has elevated people like Bandera by recognising and granting special status to the partisan army. But Bandera has proved to be an inconvenient hero.

Scholars point out that any consideration of early Ukrainian nationalists must acknowledge their record on human rights. The militant faction using Bandera's name is associated with atrocities committed towards Poles, Jews and even Ukrainians during 1943-44. For the Ukrainian nationalists, physically ridding the land of its occupiers was the way to independence. It was, of course, a time when these borderlands were subjected to terrible violence by both the Nazis and the Soviets, not to speak of decades of Polish oppression. A time when there wasn't always a clear distinction between perpetrators and victims; a time when violence was the norm. Wartime Ukraine, what historian

Timothy Snyder termed the *bloodlands*, was a victim of both the Nazis and the Soviets, a place of unimaginable horror and cruelty.

Totally against the very concept of Ukrainian statehood, the Soviets continued to make life difficult for anyone associated with the nationalists. They were branded as "unpatriotic" against the Motherland, and oppressed in ways that blighted their lives and those of their children. A woman whose nationalist grandfather had been deported told me, "We were oppressed here, at school and at university, because the Soviet ideology made us children of traitors. We were *vrag naroda*, enemies of the people."

Nowadays the partisans are officially recognised as freedom fighters. Some Ukrainians, here and in the diaspora, are wary of acknowledging the mistakes made more than seventy years ago, claiming it a continuation of Soviet brainwashing that plays into the hands of the Russians, who continue to use the partisans to justify their anti-Ukrainian propaganda. Nor have some Poles appreciated hearing the *Slava Ukraini* slogan once used by Ukrainian nationalists in wartime attacks against the Poles. It's a contentious issue, but it's hard not to sympathise with a young country struggling to piece together its history. In the words of writer Oksana Zabuzhko: Ukraine has too much overwhelming history per square metre. But Zabuzhko doesn't use that as an excuse to remain silent. Deprived of its voice for so long, she said, Ukraine is screaming out for its history to be articulated.

Some of Bandera's strongest supporters have been

among the Ukrainian diaspora in North America. In 2010, President Yushchenko awarded Bandera the title Hero of Ukraine, but the move was condemned by the European parliament and the Polish Government. Yushchenko, in a difficult position, postponed the honour and eventually it was invalidated on the grounds that the award can only be granted to a citizen of Ukraine. A convenient way to deal with an inconvenient hero.

An understanding of that past is necessary to make sense of Western Ukraine today, especially for anyone visiting L'viv's underground bunker bar. *Kriyvka*, the name meaning hideout or bunker, limits entry to those who know the old insurgents' password, although that strategy is designed to encourage visitors rather than restrict them. Opened in 2007 by the same entrepreneurial group who set up many of L'viv's quirky themed restaurants, Kriyvka is yet another controversial heritage commodity. Perhaps this one resonates a little more with the Ukrainians themselves.

The owner described the venue as having a dual function: a bar and a museum. His aim was to chip away at the Soviet-generated negative image of the partisan army. The mock underground bunker began as a serious project to educate the public about the people who'd fought for Ukraine's independence.

The first obstacle to finding Kriyvka was its address: "somewhere in Rynok Square". It took me a while to locate the right alley, at the end of which was a wooden door. Checking the password I'd written on the back of a tram ticket, I knocked.

A burly man in military uniform opened it with a stern expression. "*Slava Ukraini!*" (Glory to Ukraine!)

"*Heroyam slava*!" (Glory to the heroes!)

The man produced a tray of shots and stood aside to let me walk down into the underground bar, where a young woman in khaki barred my entrance, leading me through the same repertoire before she sat me down and handed me an English menu. It was hard to read beneath the mock gas lamps, and I went for the simple option of borshch, that iconic Ukrainian soup that comes in different shades of vegetable. In the dim light of the bunker, the one placed before me appeared to be the red version made with beetroot, served in a metal dish with a slab of bread and a jug of sour cream.

Images of wartime fighters and news cuttings were draped across the angle between ceiling and stone wall. Ancient radio equipment rotted on shelves above my head. The partisans had dug thousands of these *kriyvka* as hideouts, as bases for surprise raids, for storage and as hospitals, as well as printing centres, where booklets, training material, journals and even poetry books were produced. First built during the German occupation, these bunkers became crucial when the Soviets returned, providing shelter for Ukrainian insurgents into the 1950s. Larger bunkers could hold up to two hundred people, the smoke from their fires channelled up and out through hollow trees. People were said to emerge looking like corpses after a winter spent below ground.

The staff were enthusiastic in keeping up the pantomime. My waitress blocked the way of every new entrant with a password demand, while a man wearing a thick sheepskin waistcoat over his uniform walked around with a revolver, asking groups if there were any Muscovites among them.

The idea of entry by password has made it exceptionally popular with visitors, and the bar is open 24 hours. Were the diners genuinely interested in the Ukrainian Partisan Army? Did they buy any of the military fridge magnets and Bandera t-shirts in Kriyvka's gift shop? Had the diners any prior knowledge of partisan history and controversies, or were they here to tick off another of L'viv's oddities?

When knocking back shots of vodka with family and friends in Ukraine, I sometimes offered a tentative "*Slava Ukraini!*", to see what kind of reaction the partisan slogan generated. It always received the corresponding "*Heroyam slava!*" with a smile that suggested it was perfectly acceptable. It didn't mean the speaker held a deep-felt allegiance to the wartime partisans, or that they glorified past violence. Nor did it signify a sympathy with the far right, who in Ukraine's 2019's elections received no more than two percent of the vote. In fact, the phrase is much older than the nationalists as it goes back to a 1830s poem by Taras Shevchenko: *To Osnovyanenko*. Today it's a mainstream symbol of freedom against the Russian aggression, having become the official Euromaidan greeting during the 2013-14 student revolution. An existing slogan taken up for its convenience.

I left the bar through the gift shop, walking past a mock-Superman t-shirt where the S was for Stepan. Stepan Bandera, celebrated for what he represents today as a freedom fighter against aggression and invasion. As history is repeating itself, Ukraine takes comfort from such symbols of independence.

Young Ukrainians agreed with me when I asked about attitudes towards the partisans. "I like Stepan Bandera, and so do my friends," one young mother later told me in Kyiv. "He stood for a free and independent Ukraine, and right now it's under threat from Russia. This war is costing lives. It's costing a lot of money too," she continued. "Money that we need for developing the country. Young people here think Bandera is good."

Her next comment was prescient. "If Ukraine capitulates and allows Russia to take areas like Donbas and Crimea, what's stopping a step-by-step annexation of the rest?"

So much for the idea that Ukraine is split between east and west. As Russia revealed its true nature in 2014, the people of this young country became united, presenting their own true identity as Ukrainians. Those strips of yellow and blue represent far more than a national flag.

On my final evening I took a seat in a restaurant recommended by an English couple I'd met on one of L'viv's walking tours. Gill and Chris had been tempted by the cheap Ryanair flights to have a weekend somewhere they'd never heard of. Expecting to *rough it* in terms of food, they were astonished at finding a restaurant – *in Ukraine!* – that branded itself as Food Art, the kind of place they'd never think of visiting back in England. And if I went up to the second floor, they told me, I would not believe my eyes. They pointed out the restaurant as we walked through the main square, although Sasha, the guide, dismissed it with a wave. "That place? It's just for rich people."

Curious, that evening I walked up the stairs to be greeted by attentive staff wearing a modern take on the traditional *vyshyvanka* shirt, who led me over to a table by the window with a view of the skaters on the ice rink down in the square. But I too was being observed, by the glassy eyes of a large white reindeer strapped to the balcony outside the window.

At the other end of the room was the spectacle that Gill and Chris had alerted me to. A gigantic fish tank was set into the wall of the stairwell, spanning at least two floors. As I watched, a pair of wetsuit-clad legs entered the tank from the floor above, followed by the rest of the diver, a man who fed and played with the fish. The food quality, the wine list, the fish prodding the diver – I understood how visitors would be astonished at discovering such sophistication in a city with broken pavements and belching buses.

Could any of the ice-skating locals afford to eat here? I was used to normal Ukrainian prices now, and the cash I'd brought along was insufficient for almost every item on the menu. I ordered the cheapest dish and dismissed the wine list. When the waiter had gone, I looked back through the window and caught the mocking eye of the reindeer. I should have listened to Sasha. This place was just for rich people.

CHAPTER 7

A BUS RIDE TO THE CARPATHIAN CENTRE OF EUROPE

I CLIMBED on to the bus heading south from Ivano-Frankivsk, greeting fellow passengers with the customary

Slava Isusu Christu (Glory to Jesus Christ) and sat down, wiping the window clear of condensation. Opposite sat a young nun, an open exercise book on her lap, her smile wide with empathy towards a fellow passenger. I smiled back and took out my own notebook.

The bus filled with shoppers; older women in patterned headscarves jostled alongside younger females in baseball caps. It was September 2019 and the green and rounded Carpathians were no longer a distant set of folds on the horizon. The bus slowed down to negotiate the bends rising through pine forests, before breaking out into open pasture.

I was now in the province of Zakarpattia, formerly known as Transcarpathia, having crossed a historical boundary as well as an administrative border. Unlike Austrian Galicia, this province had lain within the Hungarian half of the Austro-Hungarian empire. The indigenous Ukrainians here saw themselves as a distinct sub-group of East Slavic people, sometimes known as Carpatho-Rusyns. On the collapse of Austria-Hungary at the end of World War 1, they found themselves living within Czechoslovakia, rather than the new interwar Poland.

Further disruption occurred during the next war when Hitler returned a southern portion of Transcarpathia to Hungary. The rest of the region became autonomous, a mini-state called Carpatho-Ukraine, where Ukrainian was, for once, the official language. Before long Hitler authorised Hungary to jump in and annexe the entire region, and Transcarpathia stayed within Hungary until 1944. Perhaps its people were lucky to avoid the wartime Soviet occupation suffered by the rest of Western Ukraine, and initially, Stalin agreed that Transcarpathia would return to Czechoslovakia after the war. Then he changed his mind, claiming the region was too ethnically Ukrainian. Better, he said, to "reunify" them with the Soviet Ukrainian Motherland. What a bitter outcome, considering these lands had never been part of Kyivan Rus', the historic union of East Slavic peoples from which evolved Ukraine, Belarus and Russia. To keep the population "pure", Stalin deported the Czechs and Slovaks to post-war Czechoslovakia.

On independence, the people of this land became hopeful of being granted self-governing status, and 78 percent of the population voted in favour of an autonomous Transcarpathia. That didn't happen either.

Almost every vehicle belching its way through Rakhiv was elderly, choking the valley with thick fumes. Warned by my friends about the town's reputation for "thieving children", I tucked my coat over my rucksack to make it less accessible and walked to the hotel I'd chosen for its "stunning views of the mountains and organisation of excursions". After last year's frustrations in Kolomiya I was hoping to get out into the Carpathians; at least the hotel could sort something for me if the trails were inadequately marked.

An expressionless young man checked me in.

"Do you have information on hiking or tours?" I asked.

"No. Just horse riding." He gestured behind his back. "There's an information office in the town."

The next two hours I crisscrossed Rakhiv, walking its length and then around its edges, not stopping or even slowing down until I found the information centre. It had concealed itself well within a hut selling souvenirs on the bank of the river Tisa. The door was locked and there was no sign of life among the fridge magnets and embroideries.

I carried on walking, past women, their legs stretched out alongside clothes and plastic bottles of milk on the pavements of a town that the Lonely Planet guide described as chaotically post-Soviet. I guessed this referred to the decaying apartment blocks juxtaposed with equally dilapidated rustic cottages. My hotel was neither chaotic nor decaying, but the white rooms and the dim corridors had no soul. The Wi-Fi worked only in the cavernous reception hall, where a sofa was placed conveniently next to the router. Unfortunately it was almost always occupied by a sprawling, phone-prodding receptionist.

Considering I was walking along a highway between L'viv and Ukraine's southern border, the traffic choking up Rakhiv all but vanished as soon as my feet left the town. A roadside cemetery held headstones bearing Hungarian names, testimony to the varied ethnicities that populate these mountainous borderlands. There'd been some tension between the Hungarians of Zakarpattia and the Ukrainian state, particularly since the 2017 reinforcement of Ukrainian as the State Language, a law brought in to strengthen the use of Ukrainian after its suppression by the Soviets. The new law was viewed as discriminatory by the Hungarian minority here, so much that Hungary itself made a formal complaint.

My walk wasn't entirely aimless. There was a Museum

of Mountain Ecology down here somewhere, and after an hour of walking a wooden board came into sight. The museum was closed for lunch, but a young man came up and unlocked the building. Guilty for disturbing his lunch break, I added my name to the visitors' book, then felt better as I noted the previous visitor's signature was dated more than a week earlier.

Occasional English signs explained the primeval character of the Carpathian woodland, a rare status supported by UNESCO. Far more entertaining were the diorama displays replicating scenes from Carpathian history, from cave dwellings to continuing traditions. Supplies of materials must have been limited at the time the dioramas were created, leading to some inventive applications of plaster to create a scene of rafting Hutsuls; pour plaster into a block, leave it to set and then hammer it, no need for precision, and bingo! You have white rapids. Add a sheet of ripped clear plastic for a "wave" of water.

Another scene depicted Malanka, the Orthodox New Year's Eve festival when villagers dress up as bears and other characters. A young man toiled through winter snow, with plaster "snowflakes" thrown over his head, turning a festive celebrator into an earthquake survivor emerging from a collapsed building. The villagers trailing behind had disguised themselves into alarmingly unhuman creatures; black goggle eyes stared above a frighteningly wide mouth, and dark facial fur encircled the face of another.

When I'd had enough, I flagged down a minibus. The driver lifted my change from a little wooden desk next to the gearstick, then drove on, leaving open the drawer stacked full of notes. So far everything contradicted the warnings I'd received that Rakhiv was a crime-ridden place.

A rider in traditional Hutsul clothing led two other horses up a lane rising into the forested hills above Rakhiv. I took the same lane, its condition worsening with every step, and fell into conversation with a man curious about the stranger following him as he limped home with his shopping. He asked why I was in Ukraine, and I explained that I'd been looking for my family. "No," he said, pointing along the lane. "Why are you here?" All I could say was that I enjoyed travelling around. He laughed at the idea that someone would come from England to this ruined lane leading nowhere.

A stream on the left had carved out a deep little gorge for itself, leaving the occupants of the houses on the other side to construct their own footbridges for access. One house, its walls covered with a vine, had neatly stencilled flowers visible through the leaves, along with a deep red zig zag border around its girth. Another house was faced with wooden shingles painted in deep stripes of blue and yellow. The colours of the fields and the sky.

Rakhiv did have a soul up here in the back lanes. It also had clean mountain air, although it wasn't until I'd turned around and walked back down into the fug of fumes that I appreciated what I'd been breathing higher up. Back at the main road I crossed it and headed uphill once more, along another decrepit lane whose crumbing surface exposed patches and kerbs of sturdy cobbles beneath.

After the track turned into the forest it crossed a steep

trail splashed with crude waymarking: large yellow arrows painted onto every other tree. They made it impossible to take a wrong turn, so I followed the trail until it opened onto a grassy track.

At last I was truly in the mountains. Rakhiv lay far below, an insignificant sprawl whose shabbiness and toxic air were obscured by the vast green folds of the Carpathians. Somewhere to the left was Hoverla, Ukraine's highest peak at 2061 metres. On the right one of the great rivers of Central Europe – the Tisa – formed a silvery ribbon, turning west to follow the international border. Behind it were layers of purple ridges marking the Maramureș region of northern Romania.

The following day I asked the bus driver for a ticket to where the 48th parallel of northern latitude crossed with the 24th of longitude, popularly known as the Centre of Europe. Sitting among the shoppers returning home from Rakhiv, I had little idea of where I should get off, just that the Centre of Europe was further down the road than I'd walked the previous day. Hemmed in by standing passengers and bags of vegetables, I could only gaze through the window as the bus slowed at a checkpoint, then sped up and sailed past the tell-tale gift shop, restaurant and car park of Europe's Centre.

Forty-five minutes later, I almost walked past the flaky blue and white pillar marking the spot where, in 1887, Austrian specialists determined this was Europe's geographical centre. Other countries had similar claims, but Ukraine was proud of this one. Of course the Soviets had been obliged to stake their own claim by erecting an ugly metal marker nearby, a double spire now defaced with stickers.

The Centre grounds were deserted but for idle stall-holders and a couple of sleeping dogs. Stalls were piled with modern mass-produced replicas of the Hutsul crafts I'd seen in Kolomiya's museum: woodcarvings, instruments and replica waistcoats. More than one item was Made in China, including something wrapped in a packet called Panda Slime.

At a time when anti-EU sentiment was raging back home in the UK, it was a relief to visit somewhere that symbolised and celebrated European unity rather than the closing of borders. With its wooden interior lit by contemporary stained-glass panels, the visitor centre exuded a sense of modernity and humanity, encouraging visitors to look at the individuals beyond broad concepts of nationality and ethnicity. Bilingual displays announced with pride that eighty-five ethnicities inhabit what's now known as Zakarpattia.

There was no obvious place from which to flag down the bus, so I walked back to the empty checkpoint and crept through, jumping when an armed guard appeared. He gestured up the road to a lay-by. I waited and waited, idling the time by watching the checkpoint. What could be the reasoning behind it? Some vehicles made a physical stop; a few merely slowed down, like my bus earlier, while other drivers sped through. It made no difference whether the guard was out on the road or inside the hut.

I waited. Each time I lifted my head, the gold patches among the forests had grown a little. Autumn was accelerating, and it was time to move on.

CHAPTER 8
TRIPPING IN BUKOVYNA

The bus struggled up the steep cobbled incline into the city of Chernivtsi, bouncing so hard that my head hit the ceiling. Twice. I'd left Zakarpattia and crossed into another former province of the Austro-Hungarian empire: Bukovyna. Unlike Galicia and Transcarpathia, Bukovyna was occupied by neither Poland nor Hungary between the wars. Instead, it was annexed by a different neighbour: Romania. The Romanians were delighted to occupy the Habsburg city Czernowitz and they renamed it Cernăuți. The Romanians claimed that Bukovyna was the birthplace of Romanian culture and they set about returning it to its roots. In their view, the Ukrainians of Bukovyna were not Ukrainians at all – they were former Romanians who'd lost the native tongue of their ancestors. Attempts to Romanise the Ukrainians were not well received.

I was still rubbing my crown as I walked up the red-carpeted steps into my hotel, an enormous Soviet-era building with extensive gardens.

That afternoon was spent idling from one café to another along Chernivtsi's long pedestrianised main street. The city's outdoor cafe culture was a dream after the rawness of Rakhiv. Its character was also distinct from that of Galician L'viv. Both cities acknowledge their shared Central European past as a pre-Soviet golden age, but Chernivtsi hadn't succumbed to quirky themed bars or "experiences" to commemorate its heritage. Here the past felt closer and less contrived, although the past was still a commodity. A statue of Franz Josef I in Shevchenko Park added to the European flavour, and back in 2008, as Chernivtsi celebrated 600 years of its founding, the city invited Karl von Habsburg as guest of honour. It's not unusual for a city to draw on the past to represent the present, and Chernivtsi does it by looking outwards, towards its neighbours in the West.

In comparison, L'viv draws on the past quite differently, with an internal reaction against the current Russian aggression. The military icons and Bandera t-shirts of the Kriyvka bunker bar seemed a more inward-looking nostalgia to reinforce Ukrainian identity. Those icons would have seemed out of place here in Chernivtsi.

In Chernivtsi, as in L'viv, the ethnic mix of the past was long gone. The Romanians, the Poles and the ethnic Germans had fled or been deported by the Soviets.

The imperial yellow building of the Museum of Local Lore had the usual gathering of under-occupied female attendants. But here the women were unusually attentive, rushing up to me as I stepped into each room, and hastening me through to the other side. Was there was something secret I wasn't allowed to see? I realised it was the opposite – they were making sure I started at the far end and missed nothing.

Chernivtsi's upheaval at the hands of its neighbours is reflected in its linguistic landscape. The language switched to match whichever occupiers moved in: from German to Romanian at the end of the First World War, then back into German under the Nazi occupation. And was it my imagination, or was there a stronger focus on World War 1 here, when the region fought on the side of the Austro-Hungarians? The exhibits from that earlier war seemed more detailed compared with those from the following decades, when the German speakers were the enemy.

How many cousins did I have here? How old was my daughter? What was the name of her dog? Was it a

Labrador? And where was my *cholovik* [husband]? One of the female staff latched onto me, asking a torrent of questions while pointing out exhibits and encouraging me to stroke the three cats who strolled around. "Follow me!" she cried and led me to another woman. "She's a university lecturer, and she has family here!" The other woman beckoned me to follow her up a staircase, along a corridor, then down another staircase to a third woman, whom she asked to unlock a doorway because *She's a university lecturer with family in Ukraine*.

The third woman unlocked a further room furnished in old Bukovyna style, with an elaborately embroidered bedspread and pillows adorning the small bed. Whoever slept there would open their eyes to looming wild boar heads and a set of deer antlers. I guessed these were more valued exhibits, kept out of reach of the hordes and their dirty fingers. My job and bloodline had elevated my trustworthiness, allowing me the privilege of wandering alone in these locked rooms.

Unlike the Lonely Planet guide to Ukraine, I wouldn't describe the buildings of Chernivtsi University, a UNESCO World Heritage Site, as "trippy". Walking around, gazing up at the arches and zigzags formed by alternating rose and crimson brickwork, there was no sense of hallucination, just awe. The roofs added further shades of green, black and blue, throwing up tall chimney-like crenelations that rose from the horizontal and the diagonal. The impression was of an elegant power station rather than a seat of learning. Nor did it look like an ecclesiastical residence, considering the latter was the original function of the university. It was the Soviets who put the official residence of the Orthodox Church leaders to a more egalitarian use when they handed it over to the city university.

Talking of acid trips, Chernivtsi's St. Nicolas Cathedral was closer to a hallucination than the elegant university. The lowering sun blushed its whitewashed walls whilst adding sparkle to the golden stars dotted over the cupola domes. Intensified against the pale sky, these deep cobalt domes sat atop four corner turrets that seemed to twist and lean in towards the central bell tower. It was as if each cupola dome were the lid on a jar, and a giant hand had attempted to wrench open the lids. As the hand twisted each dome, it knocked the turret off balance, bending it inwards.

In reality, it was an optical illusion. The turrets weren't leaning, but their slanted windows created the misconception that they were.

A short distance away was the institution that had brought me to Chernivtsi. The curator of the Museum of the Ukrainian Diaspora apologised for not speaking English, but her Ukrainian was so straightforward, and her enunciation so clear, that I understood close to half of what she said.

The earliest wave of emigration from Bukovyna was pre-World War 1, mostly to Canada. The second wave took place when the Romanians came in and attempted to "liberate" the Ukrainians from their language. The third wave fled during the Stalinist years of repression. And just as a wave ebbs and flows, so does migration, although these days it was rare for the original migrants themselves to return. Instead, it's us children or grandchildren who come home, digging out the phantoms when we realise we've left it too late to ask questions of our parents. Like the man who'd left a comment in the visitor book, saying he'd "welled up" when he saw a photograph of his uncle on the museum display.

The two women staff members were wishing me goodbye when I pulled up at a pair of leather shoes in a cabinet, identical to those I'd worn as a child. I couldn't remember where my own had come from – in one of the parcels from "Russia", perhaps? Every detail was identical, from the ridge of plaited leather running from the pointed toe, to the threading along the sides and the carvings on either side of the plait. "I had shoes like this when I was a child!"

The women frowned. It was unlikely, as the shoes were a relic from the past, an antique. These were Hutsul shoes, known as *postoli*, an endangered craft. Only one professional *postoli* maker remained, in the Carpathian town of Kosmach.

It wasn't until I found the Polish version, *kierpce*, for sale online that I understood. This style of shoe had been worn by mountain dwellers right across the Carpathians, including the Górale in nearby Poland. My father must have bought me modern replicas when he visited Poland. I need not reproach myself for having lost a precious antique. I could buy a replacement from the Internet.

. . .

A German coach tour filled the hotel restaurant. There was no menu that night, but I was allowed to join the smartly dressed Germans and eat from their buffet at a small price. I asked the waiter for a glass of wine.

"You have to go to the bar for wine, not here in the restaurant."

I waited at the bar until a woman finally turned up.

"We don't have wine here. Go to the restaurant."

Back at my table, I caught the eye of a passing waiter, who nodded and walked over to a couple on an adjacent table. He picked up the couple's open bottle and brought it over to my table, where he lifted my glass. Not surprisingly, the couple called out in protest, glaring at me. What was going on? Was this some archaic communist ideal, whereby a scruffy-looking single female was granted a share of the wine from the bottle of wealthier others?

I kept my eyes lowered as the waiter returned the bottle to the fuming couple, and eventually another waiter brought over my own glass of white. It cost twice the price of the buffet.

CHAPTER 9

REFORGING THE BONDS OF OUR ANCESTORS: KYIV IN DECEMBER

People in Western Ukraine were surprised that I hadn't visited Kyiv. It was true that Western Ukraine had been a magnet for me ever since I set foot there, one reason being that it was where my father's family were from.

But I had an idea that going further east would help me understand the west. You get a different perspective on something by seeing what it isn't. In the summer of 2019 I'd stayed in Western Ukraine with Yuliya, the niece of my father's late Ukrainian wife, and she'd assured me that if I went to Kyiv, her sister and her niece would meet me. I'd booked a flight there and then.

Ruslana, a Kyiv-born nurse working in England, sat next to me on the plane and asked me what I was planning to do. She nodded with enthusiasm until I mentioned my plan to ride tram number 12 through the forest north of Kyiv. Her eyes rounded in horror as she told me a former neighbour had been found dead in the woods near her dacha. "It was in the news in England!" she said. Ruslana made me promise I wouldn't get off the tram.

That evening, I put on my brave face and walked out into night-time Kyiv, heading for Khreshchatyk, Kyiv's central road. Used to L'viv's cobbled squares and Central European heritage, I stood immobile with panic as Khreshchatyk turned out to be an 8-lane highway overshadowed by tall Soviet architecture. Doormen stood outside clubs, and groups of men loitered in the cold darkness. The towering hulks along Khreshchatyk reminded me that Kyiv had been under Soviet influence for far longer than Western Ukraine. A survey from 2005 indicated that some Central Ukrainians felt more kindred towards Russians than to the

Western Ukrainians. That, of course, was well before Russia invaded in 2014.

The following morning, as I waited by the metro exit, I opened my bag to check the black and white photograph that had broken the ice on that first visit to my father's village: Olena as the young mother standing with her children Yuliya, Andriy and Katya. My father's in-laws. And now I recognised Katya as she emerged at the top of the subway stairs, her adult expression little changed from that in the photograph. With Katya was her English-speaking daughter, Nataliya.

Katya and I linked arms after she tugged up my hood, a gesture she continued to do throughout the week. Walking back to my hotel at night, alone, a phantom hand would tug at my hood as her voice echoed in my head. "Stay warm, Michelle!"

We walked along Khreshchatyk towards a soaring metal arch built by the Soviets to symbolise their friendship with Ukraine. Today the arch was defiled by a jagged black sticker, a metaphorical crack representing the rift caused by Russia holding Ukrainian political prisoners. I walked back a little to capture it with Katya and Nataliya silhouetted in the centre as they gazed up at the apex. Today we were bridging a more personal divide: the barrier wrought by the Iron Curtain.

"Some people want to pull down the arch,' said Nataliya. She shrugged. "I don't, not really. It's part of our history."

. . .

Glass panels formed a walkway high above the riverbank with a giddying view down to the Dnipro, the great river that flows through Kyiv on its way from Russia and Belarus to the Black Sea. On the opposite bank, grey and brown winter woodland dotted with dachas stretched towards a skyline of apartment blocks. One of those blocks was where I'd be eating tonight.

Artists stood around rubbing their hands. No one was looking at the paintings of Carpathian houses and the number 12 tram gliding through the glorious autumn forest.

"Do you like this kind of thing?" asked Nataliya.

I nodded. "I do some painting myself. I paint landscapes." I had a photograph on my phone of the painting I'd done the previous Sunday. "Here's one of the hayricks in the Carpathians."

Nataliya bent over with laughter at the idea that a foreigner would paint something so banal. "Don't you have these things in English fields?"

We carried on down the steep cobbles of Andriyvski Uzviz, past stalls perched awkwardly on the sloping pavements, the tables dotted with tourist souvenirs and war memorabilia. At the bottom of the street stood the Kyiv Ferris wheel, motionless at the edge of Kontraktova Square. "We've never been on it," said Nataliya. Katya said something, and Nataliya laughed. "Mom is afraid to go on it! Do you want to?"

I nodded. "If you like, but it doesn't look open."

A couple of men were working on its inners. Nataliya spoke with one of them, then turned to beckon us. "It doesn't run in the mornings, but they're opening it for us," she explained. I hoped the work they were doing wasn't critical in any mechanical aspects.

As the cabin rose, the view opened out over Podil, the city's riverside port, and an Orthodox Church rose in every direction. I was beginning to understand Kyiv's topography; even at the highest point of the wheel, it felt as if we were below everything else except the banks of the Dnipro.

I stood to take photographs, which alarmed my hosts. They were astounded to hear that the London Eye was four times higher than this one. Katya's eyes widened at the idea of riding something four times as terrifying.

Beneath the stained glass and gold arches of the funicular entrance we bought tickets for a ride back to higher ground. Emerging at St Michael's Golden-Domed monastery, I blinked as powder blue walls melted into an identical shade of winter sky. Gilded cupolas darkened the cobbles with long midwinter shadows. In November 2013, more than a hundred Euromaidan protestors had barricaded themselves behind these monastery walls. The students had been pursued for their "crime" of hampering the decoration of the square's New Year tree.

Today, it was a peaceful haven of blue and gold. A long wall painted with angels and saints led us towards a metro station, where fast elevators made hesitation fatal. At Zoloti Vorota station we waited for the train alongside locals who gazed without expression at the tracks, while I tipped my head back, mesmerised by the ribbons of mosaic curving beneath a succession of chandeliers.

Up again we went, emerging into suburbs doused by the chill of an approaching winter evening. This was Pozniaky, an established community on the edge of Kyiv. Almost all the older houses had been demolished to make way for vertical living; modern apartments were interspersed with Soviet blocks, all tinged pink as the lowering sun cast its spell. Katya led us into an old block, its dark green paintwork dulled and chipped over the decades. Tiptoeing past an elderly concierge asleep in a sentry box, we rode the tiny elevator up 14 floors and stepped into the apartment with its little covered balcony, the windows netted with wire to stop the cat leaping out. Katya gestured towards the man at the stove. "Petro does the cooking, not me," she said, wrinkling up her nose. "I prefer to clean."

Petro served up chickpea soup followed by mashed potato and gherkins, and carved through a slab of the salted pork fat known as *salo*. I'd seen chunks of this strange white food for sale, available natural as well as herbed, spiced or salted. It went well with the mashed potato.

Petro fired a string of British icons at me, curious to hear my opinion of Queen Elizabeth, Winston Churchill and Princess Diana. But things the rest of the world judge us by are often of little interest to those of us who live there, and I struggled to come up with answers. I had more to say about wages, the cost of a house and that old chestnut, the retirement pension. Their eyes widened as my figures made retired Britons sound wealthy. How to put it into context? I gave a few rental costs and explained that Britain's wealth is shockingly uneven. I compared the streets of Kyiv with the cities of England, where doorways are increasingly occupied by the homeless. I explained that in some poorer areas, teachers now bring food and even clothing in for the children. That a growing number of British families – working people – rely on the generosity of donations to food banks.

They shook their heads. This wasn't the vision they had. They understood the concept of a food bank, but in England?

"Is it ruled by oligarchs?" asked Nataliya. I laughed, then thought about what I'd been describing. It was a good question. Oligarchs hold power over political parties and the media, but in the conventional definition, the monopolies are dependent on state money rather than the usual business competition. So officially, no.

"We have a sovereign parliament, but certain people use their vast wealth to influence national politics. And when wealthy people buy up the media, they can manipulate the nation to think and vote a certain way."

Nataliya's three-year-old son turned up, clutching his English homework, a poem about winter that I just about translated back into his mother tongue. This three-year-old's English was better than my Ukrainian.

A ticket for the tram ride into the forest cost an equivalent of 25p for the 75-minute journey. As the number 12 tram left the city centre it passed a line of people sitting at the roadside, their goods spread across blankets. Here, as in other street markets I'd seen in Ukraine, the things being sold often defied an attempt to name or categorise them. Apartment blocks loomed up on both sides. New buildings dwarfed the older Soviet ones in width and height, especially the five-storey *Khrushchevka*, Nikita Khrushchev's solution to the post-war housing crisis. The Soviets built this distinctive blueprint of low-rise, low-cost, brick-built apartments across the cities of the former USSR. Showing ominous cracks along the joints of the protruding balconies, Khrushchev's temporary solution had clearly surpassed its use-by date here in Kyiv.

Shoppers wedged themselves into the aisle of the tram, distended bags around their feet. One by one they stepped down and waddled off towards their apartments. By the time we entered the forest, around a dozen of us were left on the tram.

Bare winter trees made a mesmerising tableau, enlivened only by the odd patch of snow and a dog sniffing among dried leaves. It was a perfect setting for a horror movie. No doubt the greenery of summer and the vividness of autumn make it inviting at other times of the year, but today I was happy to heed Ruslana's advice. At one point, a couple got off at a metal shelter and looked around them with bemusement. I wanted to bang on the window and tell them to get back on the tram.

When the tram emerged from the forest, the flash of daylight snapped me awake and I pressed the buzzer; the tram stopped, and the door opened, just for me, on the edge of a park manicured out of the forest. Women pushed toddlers down to a frozen lake. An elaborate new timber bridge spanned the water, and an elderly couple walked across it and disappeared among the trees. *Don't go into the forest!* I wanted to shout at them. Instead, I turned around and ran towards the small band of people waiting by the tram tracks.

Each Kyiv metro station is gloriously distinct. Close to where I was staying was Teatralna, the venue for a weekly

Saturday Night Dance down in the metro station. By chance, I happened to come through it that Saturday evening, and stopped, entranced by the couples dancing to live musicians, right there in the entrance hall. Longing to join them, I could only watch as the couples swirled each other around the metro station floor. "It's a regular thing – the Saturday night disco for old people!" said Nataliya.

That evening Katya and I sat together in the small kitchen, post-borshch. Katya wasn't a blood relative, and she had never met my father – he would have been her uncle by marriage, although he'd left the village, in what had then been Soviet-occupied Poland, some twenty years before she'd even been born. And I'd grown up not even knowing this family of in-laws existed. But as Katya and I sat knocking back Sauvignon as if it were shots of vodka, our simple communication supplemented by guesswork, the bond between us was extraordinary. Katya nailed it in a single sentence when she said our late fathers would have been happy to see us sitting at her kitchen table.

My father had sent enough photographs to his in-laws to ensure they knew about his English family. The photographs the in-laws sent to us, on the other hand, sat in a shoebox, until I became haunted by the faces almost fifty years later. But he would have been happy to see us closing the divide. It hardly mattered that we weren't blood relatives; our friendship was rooted in the bonds of our ancestors.

. . .

I asked Katya about the Russian I heard spoken in Kyiv, such as the *da* for "yes", rather than the *tak* of Western Ukraine.

She nodded. "Not everyone can speak Ukrainian." The Soviets had imposed Russian as the language of education and of cities such as Kyiv, resulting in a steady decline in the percentage of people claiming Ukrainian as their mother tongue. She laughed. "I don't speak Ukrainian properly!" She explained how her sister in Western Ukraine didn't either. "Yuliya speaks a mixture. Ukrainian, Polish, Austrian." Katya was referring to what some call the Galician dialect. My teacher Xenia had told me a few archaic words derived from German at the time of the Austro-Hungarian Empire; words that were still spoken in Western Ukraine. Not to forget the influx of Polish words from the former rulers and settlers.

After decades of imposing Russian with varied results across the country, Ukraine is a context where language variety doesn't always correspond with identity. Katya identified, unequivocally, as Ukrainian, but after forty years in Kyiv, she claimed only partial competence in Ukrainian language. When she went back to the village, her family spoke another variety, one peppered with archaic words unfamiliar to Ukrainians living further east.

And *Sujhyk*? Katya nodded. A blend of Ukrainian and Russian, *Sujhyk* mixed the rules and the meanings of both languages, making it difficult to understand.

I pulled on my boots to walk to the metro. Petro pointed at them. "Clean?"

I nodded. Yes, I'd cleaned my boots before I left the UK.

He pointed again, grinning. They were shining as never

before. I looked back up at Petro, bent over with laughter. "I cleaned Katya's boots, so I did yours as well."

The following day Katya and I walked towards a cluster of gold and turquoise on the wooded slopes above the Dnipro, a maze of churches and bell towers that formed Kyivo-Pechers'ka Lavra, one of four senior monasteries (lavra) in Ukraine. Way back in 11th-century Kyivan Rus', this monastery was the historic centre of Orthodox Christianity. For around half of Katya's life, the complex had been a Soviet "House of Recreation", its cathedral used as a cinema.

Katya opened the heavy doors of church after church, handing notes to the candle sellers, and receiving long, thin tapers that we lit and planted into holders. Puffing, she led me up the twisting staircase of the Great Bell Tower to a platform below the gilded dome. Only now, looking down, did I understand the vast complex, divided into Upper and Lower Lavra, linked by covered walkways and steep cobbled paths. Beneath them was a labyrinth of caves.

We descended into the nearer caves, long tunnels whose narrow corridors were barely wide enough to squeeze past other people holding lit candles. Candle smoke and incense scented the dark air, mixed with a fustiness that I dared not think about too deeply. The tunnels are the resting places of monks whose bodies were left to mummify in the cold, dry air; a natural process that was interpreted as a miracle. And here was the first mummified monk, dimly illuminated in an alcove within a glass-topped cabinet, the body clothed in an embroidered robe. Katya bent to kiss the glass covering.

The vision of her lips touching the glass, where thousands of others had done, flashed into my uneasy mind just three months later when the world came to a halt during the Covid-19 epidemic.

The following day I met Katya to walk to Kyiv's National Museum of the History of Ukraine in the Second World War. The enormous brutalist sculptures lining the underpass were an uneasy reminder of who built this museum. But even they were overshadowed by the towering metal statue of the Mother of the Nation (*Rodina Mat*), another Soviet-built monument, although back then the "nation" was the USSR. Erected by Brezhnev in 1981, the Rodina Mat presents a conundrum in the face of Ukraine's recent decommunisation laws. Ideally, the Soviet emblem would be removed from the Mother's shield and replaced with the Ukrainian *tryzub* (trident). But that would be a costly and difficult feat; Ukraine has more pressing issues to deal with. On the other hand, the Mother presents an opportunity for Ukrainians to reinterpret the Mother's gaze to suit the times. Originally placed so that she gazed appreciatively towards the former Soviet "motherland", that gaze is now perceived as a Ukrainian stare of defiance towards Moscow.

Only a tiny percentage of visitors complete the complicated trip up the length of the structure to stand on a giddying viewing platform at the level of the Mother's shield. An inclined elevator carries people from the shoulder to the elbow, after which visitors must then climb, harnessed, up narrow vertical tubes that are open only to those who are sufficiently slim. And skirts are expressly forbidden.

The war museum itself sits inside the Soviet statue's pedestal, whose circular base introduces visitors to a more contemporary war: the conflict on Ukraine's eastern borders. Only after viewing that section can the visitor move back in time to the original Soviet purpose of the museum: visual reminders of the Nazi occupation, such as a bone-crushing machine and a pair of gloves made from human skin.

Despite the Soviets constructing the museum to glorify what they prefer to call their Great Patriotic War, that purpose has been nicely subverted since independence. Today the museum's underlying narrative is that the conflict never really ended for Ukraine in 1945. Everywhere, visitors are reminded that Ukraine remained occupied and repressed by a totalitarian Soviet regime.

The top floor, titled the Unfinished War, carried a stark and prophetic warning against those who have already begun to redraw the map of Europe while neglecting the lessons of history. Photograph albums lay open to show Ukrainian deportees working in the hostile conditions of Siberia. Other images showed non-Ukrainians expelled into Poland. These were people who often moved into the Silesian homes of similarly deported Germans, their former occupants having moved west as their homeland became Poland. Some deportees managed to come back. Others, like my cousin, were forced to live out their lives separated from their roots.

A vast table curved down the centre of the final gallery, its places set for the eternally absent. Empty glasses alongside death notification letters symbolised these lost others. As Katya and I walked down, thousands of eyes followed us from the wall on one side, while the faces of their widows stared from the opposite wall. In the corner sat the abandoned instruments of a phantom brass band.

What a poignant example it was of *show don't tell*, that technique employed by writers to avoid a mechanical disclosure. No descriptive placards were necessary. Instead, each observer was left to make an active interpretation through their own experiences.

Kyiv generated a sadness that proved difficult to shake off. I felt it especially whenever I left Katya's apartment and walked with her to the metro, turning back to wave to her as she stood behind the ticket barriers, wrapped against the cold in her black padded coat. Perhaps it was a sense of what was coming. Whatever sparked it, apprehension descended around me whenever I said goodbye.

Kyiv also deepened my resolve to spend more time in Western Ukraine. I'd come to Kyiv to gain a clearer perspective of the borderlands, hoping to understand Western Ukraine by seeing what it wasn't. And that aim had worked, whereby Kyiv intensified my own conversation with the western lands. I missed L'viv, with its quirky restaurants, its Central European squares and the ease of melting into the city. In L'viv, I comfortably straddled the intersection of outsider and insider. Western Ukraine was, after all, where my roots lay. Some say that a place can be in your DNA from generations of your ancestors; traces linger from the soil, the food grown there, the water. I don't know if there's a credible science behind this.

But psychologically, there's much to be said for filling the gaps in the family narrative. Those monochrome others in the photographs were people like us; they just happened to be shaped by different circumstances.

In the timeless words of Nicolas Bouvier, "You think you are making a trip, but soon it is making you – or unmaking you."

AFTERWORD

Please consider donating to help Ukraine's people during this brutal and senseless invasion.

There are many options, including large international organisations. But you can also donate to a Ukrainian organisation and send your money to those on the ground, such as Caritas Ukraine and Razom's Emergency Response. If you'd like to donate towards protective gear and other equipment for the Ukrainian Armed Forces, go to Come Back Alive.

ABOUT THE AUTHOR

Born in the English Midlands, Michelle Lawson lives in south-west England and works as a lecturer in Applied Linguistics. Her interest in how place can be a portal to understanding ourselves is a theme in her writing.

More information and articles can be found at: www.michelle-lawson.com and at www.medlartree.com

If you've enjoyed this book, please consider leaving a short review on your favourite bookstore or book review site.

Sign up to Michelle's occasional mailing list for updates on new writing, and receive a short story set in the Ariège Pyrenees: *Unimaginable Times*: woman investigating her family history finds herself uncomfortably close to the past.

Click on the book or follow the link to: https://www.subscribepage.com/medlartree-landing-page.

You can also sign up at www.medlartree.com.

facebook.com/MichelleLawsonWrites

twitter.com/MichelleLawson_

instagram.com/michelle.lawson.writes

ALSO BY MICHELLE LAWSON

A House at the End of the Track: Travels Among the English in the Ariège Pyrenees

Intrigued by a scattered English community in the French Pyrenees, Michelle Lawson travels around interviewing Britons living in the remote Ariège department. *A House at the End of the Track* is an intriguing tapestry of the hopes, dreams and reality of life in France, in English.

Adapted from an original academic study, the book is also a celebration of this wild and depopulated corner of Europe.

The Wicked Game

Michelle's fiction is inspired by her observations of people and place. Themes of manipulation and vulnerability, and the difficulty of separating a dream from reality, are what inspired her debut novel, *The Wicked Game*, set in Kathmandu, Nepal.

The Way Things Are Out Here: Five Travel Tales

From obsession with a stranger on Instagram, to the sexual dynamics on a coach holiday, the characters in these stories are all driven by a desire to belong when they find themselves in unfamiliar places. Some seek friendship, some romance. Others are following the dream of a new life abroad. Join them in France, Germany and the Carpathians as they discover the way things really are out there.

Includes a bonus travel memoir: *Finding the Wrong Family in Western Ukraine.*

Printed in Poland
by Amazon Fulfillment
Poland Sp. z o.o., Wrocław

89357475R00056